KU-342-067

| | | |
|---|---|---|
| 0 x 7 = 0 | 0 x 8 = | 0 x |
| 1 x 7 = 7 | 1 x 8 = | 1 x |
| 2 x 7 = 14 | 2 x 8 = 16 | 2 x 9 = 18 |
| 3 x 7 = 21 | 3 x 8 = 24 | 3 x 9 = 27 |
| 4 x 7 = 28 | 4 x 8 = 32 | 4 x 9 = 36 |
| 5 x 7 = 35 | 5 x 8 = 40 | 5 x 9 = 45 |
| 6 x 7 = 42 | 6 x 8 = 48 | 6 x 9 = 54 |
| 7 x 7 = 49 | 7 x 8 = 56 | 7 x 9 = 63 |
| 8 x 7 = 56 | 8 x 8 = 64 | 8 x 9 = 72 |
| 9 x 7 = 63 | 9 x 8 = 72 | 9 x 9 = 81 |
| 10 x 7 = 70 | 10 x 8 = 80 | 10 x 9 = 90 |
| 11 x 7 = 77 | 11 x 8 = 88 | 11 x 9 = 99 |
| 12 x 7 = 84 | 12 x 8 = 96 | 12 x 9 = 108 |

| | | |
|---|---|---|
| 0 x 10 = 0 | 0 x 11 = 0 | 0 x 12 = 0 |
| 1 x 10 = 10 | 1 x 11 = 11 | 1 x 12 = 12 |
| 2 x 10 = 20 | 2 x 11 = 22 | 2 x 12 = 24 |
| 3 x 10 = 30 | 3 x 11 = 33 | 3 x 12 = 36 |
| 4 x 10 = 40 | 4 x 11 = 44 | 4 x 12 = 48 |
| 5 x 10 = 50 | 5 x 11 = 55 | 5 x 12 = 60 |
| 6 x 10 = 60 | 6 x 11 = 66 | 6 x 12 = 72 |
| 7 x 10 = 70 | 7 x 11 = 77 | 7 x 12 = 84 |
| 8 x 10 = 80 | 8 x 11 = 88 | 8 x 12 = 96 |
| 9 x 10 = 90 | 9 x 11 = 99 | 9 x 12 = 108 |
| 10 x 10 = 100 | 10 x 11 = 110 | 10 x 12 = 120 |
| 11 x 10 = 110 | 11 x 11 = 121 | 11 x 12 = 132 |
| 12 x 10 = 120 | 12 x 11 = 132 | 12 x 12 = 144 |

## MESSAGE TO PARENTS

These books are designed to help children in the 6-8 age range to learn and practice their early maths skills. Basic facts about addition, subtraction, multiplication and division are presented in a clear and understandable way with the use of amusing, colourful pictures, simple text and numerous games and puzzles. In this way the books can be used in the home to complement and reinforce the educational process that takes place in school.

Knowledge absorbed gradually is usually absorbed more thoroughly, so never try to cover too much in one session. It is important to make sure that your child understands each page as you progress together through the books. Always remember that learning ought to be an enjoyable experience and, in particular, that maths can be and should be FUN.

First published 1995 by Brown Watson
The Old Mill, Fleckney Road
Kibworth Beauchamp, Leics LE8 0HG
© 1995 Brown Watson
ISBN: 0-7097-1085-2

# times tables

Compiled by Colin Clark
Illustrated by Stephen Holmes

# 3 × 3

**Brown Watson**
ENGLAND

# 2 times table

| | | | | |
|---|---|---|---|---|
| 0 | × | 2 | = | 0 |
| 1 | × | 2 | = | 2 |
| 2 | × | 2 | = | 4 |
| 3 | × | 2 | = | 6 |
| 4 | × | 2 | = | 8 |
| 5 | × | 2 | = | 10 |
| 6 | × | 2 | = | 12 |
| 7 | × | 2 | = | 14 |
| 8 | × | 2 | = | 16 |
| 9 | × | 2 | = | 18 |
| 10 | × | 2 | = | 20 |
| 11 | × | 2 | = | 22 |
| 12 | × | 2 | = | 24 |

Jack has 2 balloons.　　　John has 2 balloons.

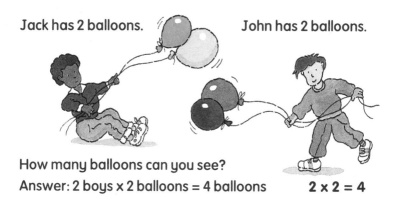

How many balloons can you see?

Answer: 2 boys x 2 balloons = 4 balloons　　　**2 x 2 = 4**

---

Jane has 2 gloves.　Jenny has 2 gloves.　Jill has 2 gloves.

There are 3 girls. Each girl has 2 gloves.

How many gloves can you see?

Answer: 3 girls x 2 gloves = 6 gloves　　　**3 x 2 = 6**

---

Here are 2 girls, Jane and Jenny. Each girl has 3 gloves.

How many gloves can you see?

Answer: 2 girls x 3 gloves = 6 gloves　　　**2 x 3 = 6**

**2 x 3 = 6 is the same as 3 x 2 = 6**

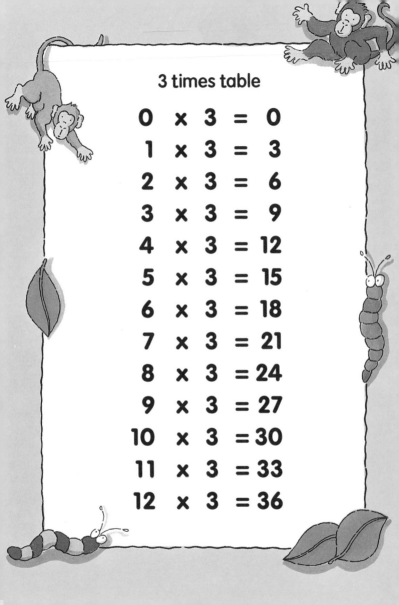

# 3 times table

| | | | | |
|---|---|---|---|---|
| 0 | × | 3 | = | 0 |
| 1 | × | 3 | = | 3 |
| 2 | × | 3 | = | 6 |
| 3 | × | 3 | = | 9 |
| 4 | × | 3 | = | 12 |
| 5 | × | 3 | = | 15 |
| 6 | × | 3 | = | 18 |
| 7 | × | 3 | = | 21 |
| 8 | × | 3 | = | 24 |
| 9 | × | 3 | = | 27 |
| 10 | × | 3 | = | 30 |
| 11 | × | 3 | = | 33 |
| 12 | × | 3 | = | 36 |

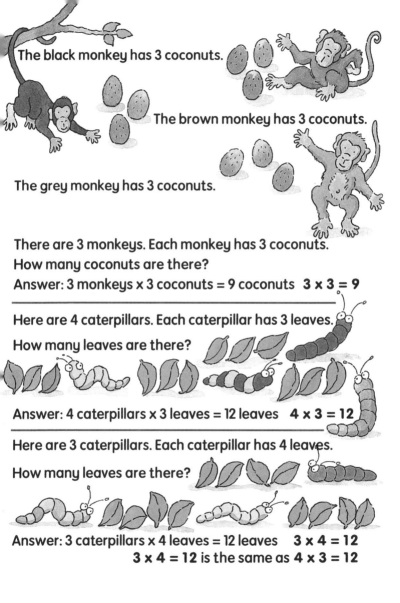

The black monkey has 3 coconuts.

The brown monkey has 3 coconuts.

The grey monkey has 3 coconuts.

There are 3 monkeys. Each monkey has 3 coconuts.
How many coconuts are there?
Answer: 3 monkeys x 3 coconuts = 9 coconuts  **3 x 3 = 9**

Here are 4 caterpillars. Each caterpillar has 3 leaves.

How many leaves are there?

Answer: 4 caterpillars x 3 leaves = 12 leaves  **4 x 3 = 12**

Here are 3 caterpillars. Each caterpillar has 4 leaves.

How many leaves are there?

Answer: 3 caterpillars x 4 leaves = 12 leaves  **3 x 4 = 12**
**3 x 4 = 12** is the same as **4 x 3 = 12**

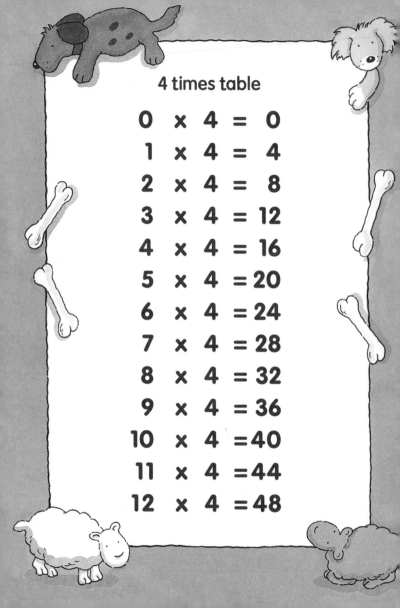

# 4 times table

| | | | | |
|---|---|---|---|---|
| 0 | × | 4 | = | 0 |
| 1 | × | 4 | = | 4 |
| 2 | × | 4 | = | 8 |
| 3 | × | 4 | = | 12 |
| 4 | × | 4 | = | 16 |
| 5 | × | 4 | = | 20 |
| 6 | × | 4 | = | 24 |
| 7 | × | 4 | = | 28 |
| 8 | × | 4 | = | 32 |
| 9 | × | 4 | = | 36 |
| 10 | × | 4 | = | 40 |
| 11 | × | 4 | = | 44 |
| 12 | × | 4 | = | 48 |

The black sheep has 4 legs.

The white sheep has 4 legs.

The grey sheep has 4 legs.

The sheep with horns has 4 legs.

There are 4 sheep. Each sheep has 4 legs.

How many legs can you see?

Answer: 4 sheep x 4 legs = 16 legs          **4 x 4 = 16**

Here are 5 dogs. Each dog has 4 bones.

How many bones are there?

Answer: 5 dogs x 4 bones = 20 bones          **5 x 4 = 20**

Here are 4 dogs. Each dog has 5 bones.

How many bones are there?

Answer: 4 dogs x 5 bones = 20 bones          **4 x 5 = 20**

 **4 x 5 = 20** is the same as **5 x 4 = 20**

# 5 times table

| | | | | |
|---|---|---|---|---|
| 0 | × | 5 | = | 0 |
| 1 | × | 5 | = | 5 |
| 2 | × | 5 | = | 10 |
| 3 | × | 5 | = | 15 |
| 4 | × | 5 | = | 20 |
| 5 | × | 5 | = | 25 |
| 6 | × | 5 | = | 30 |
| 7 | × | 5 | = | 35 |
| 8 | × | 5 | = | 40 |
| 9 | × | 5 | = | 45 |
| 10 | × | 5 | = | 50 |
| 11 | × | 5 | = | 55 |
| 12 | × | 5 | = | 60 |

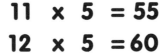

The white mouse has 5 pieces of cheese.

The black mouse has 5 pieces of cheese.

The grey mouse has 5 pieces of cheese.

The brown mouse has 5 pieces of cheese.

The spotted mouse has 5 pieces of cheese.

There are 5 mice. Each mouse has 5 pieces of cheese.
How many pieces of cheese are there?

Answer:   5 mice x 5 pieces of cheese =
25 pieces of cheese                    **5 x 5 = 25**

---

Here are 6 cats. Each cat has 5 kittens.

How many kittens are there?
Answer: 6 cats x 5 kittens = 30 kittens

**6 x 5 = 30**
**6 x 5 = 30** is the same as **5 x 6 = 30**

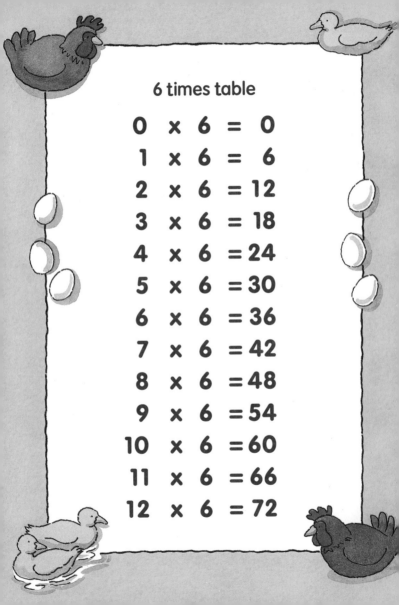

# 6 times table

| | | | | |
|---|---|---|---|---|
| 0 | × | 6 | = | 0 |
| 1 | × | 6 | = | 6 |
| 2 | × | 6 | = | 12 |
| 3 | × | 6 | = | 18 |
| 4 | × | 6 | = | 24 |
| 5 | × | 6 | = | 30 |
| 6 | × | 6 | = | 36 |
| 7 | × | 6 | = | 42 |
| 8 | × | 6 | = | 48 |
| 9 | × | 6 | = | 54 |
| 10 | × | 6 | = | 60 |
| 11 | × | 6 | = | 66 |
| 12 | × | 6 | = | 72 |

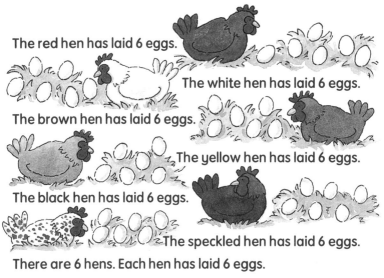

The red hen has laid 6 eggs.

The white hen has laid 6 eggs.

The brown hen has laid 6 eggs.

The yellow hen has laid 6 eggs.

The black hen has laid 6 eggs.

The speckled hen has laid 6 eggs.

There are 6 hens. Each hen has laid 6 eggs.

How many eggs can you see?

Answer: 6 hens x 6 eggs = 36 eggs          **6 x 6 = 36**

---

There are 7 ducks and each duck has 6 ducklings.

How many ducklings are there?

Answer: 7 ducks x 6 ducklings = 42 ducklings          **7 x 6 = 42**

---

There are 6 ducks and each
duck has 7 ducklings.

How many ducklings are there?

Answer: 6 ducks x 7 ducklings = 42 ducklings

**6 x 7 = 42**

**6 x 7 = 42** is the same as **7 x 6 = 42**

# 7 times table

$$0 \times 7 = 0$$
$$1 \times 7 = 7$$
$$2 \times 7 = 14$$
$$3 \times 7 = 21$$
$$4 \times 7 = 28$$
$$5 \times 7 = 35$$
$$6 \times 7 = 42$$
$$7 \times 7 = 49$$
$$8 \times 7 = 56$$
$$9 \times 7 = 63$$
$$10 \times 7 = 70$$
$$11 \times 7 = 77$$
$$12 \times 7 = 84$$

The brown puppy has 7 balls.

The black puppy has 7 balls.

The white puppy has 7 balls.

The golden puppy has 7 balls.

The shaggy puppy has 7 balls.

The small puppy has 7 balls.

The biggest puppy has 7 balls.

There are 7 puppies. Each puppy has 7 balls.

How many balls are there?

Answer: 7 puppies x 7 balls = 49 balls          **7 x 7 = 49**

---

There are 8 frogs and each frog has 7 tadpoles.

How many tadpoles are there?

Answer: 8 frogs x 7 tadpoles = 56 tadpoles          **8 x 7 = 56**

**8 x 7 = 56** is the same as **7 x 8 = 56**

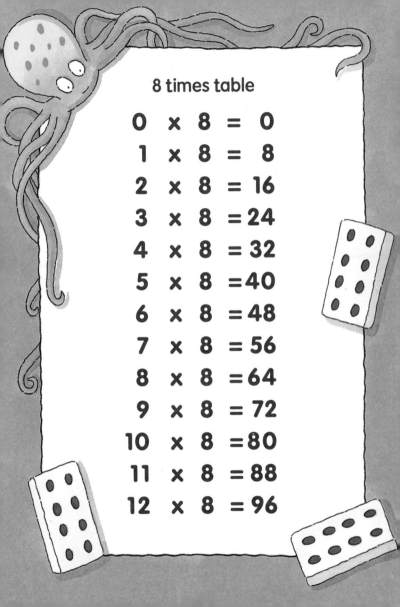

# 8 times table

| | | | | |
|---:|:---:|:---:|:---:|---:|
| 0 | × | 8 | = | 0 |
| 1 | × | 8 | = | 8 |
| 2 | × | 8 | = | 16 |
| 3 | × | 8 | = | 24 |
| 4 | × | 8 | = | 32 |
| 5 | × | 8 | = | 40 |
| 6 | × | 8 | = | 48 |
| 7 | × | 8 | = | 56 |
| 8 | × | 8 | = | 64 |
| 9 | × | 8 | = | 72 |
| 10 | × | 8 | = | 80 |
| 11 | × | 8 | = | 88 |
| 12 | × | 8 | = | 96 |

The octopus has eight arms.

Here are another 7 octopuses. Each one has 8 arms.

There are 8 octopuses. Each octopus has 8 arms.

How many arms are there?

Answer: 8 octopuses x 8 arms = 64 arms      **8 x 8 = 64**

---

Here are 9 dominoes. Each domino has 8 spots on it.

How many spots can you see?

Answer: 9 dominoes x 8 spots = 72 spots      **9 x 8 = 72**

**9 x 8 = 72** is the same as **8 x 9 = 72**

# 9 times table

| | | | | |
|---|---|---|---|---|
| 0 | × | 9 | = | 0 |
| 1 | × | 9 | = | 9 |
| 2 | × | 9 | = | 18 |
| 3 | × | 9 | = | 27 |
| 4 | × | 9 | = | 36 |
| 5 | × | 9 | = | 45 |
| 6 | × | 9 | = | 54 |
| 7 | × | 9 | = | 63 |
| 8 | × | 9 | = | 72 |
| 9 | × | 9 | = | 81 |
| 10 | × | 9 | = | 90 |
| 11 | × | 9 | = | 99 |
| 12 | × | 9 | = | 108 |

The flower has 9 petals on it.

Here are another 8 flowers.

Each flower has 9 petals.

There are 9 flowers. Each flower has 9 petals.

How many petals can you see?

Answer: 9 flowers x 9 petals = 81 petals        **9 x 9 = 81**

---

Here are 10 crates. Each crate has 9 lemonade bottles in it.

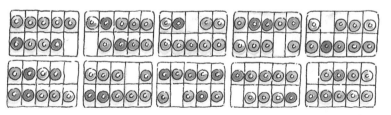

How many lemonade bottles are there?

Answer: 10 crates x 9 bottles = 90 bottles    **10 x 9 = 90**
                      **10 x 9 = 90** is the same as **9 x 10 = 90**

# 10 times table

| | | | | |
|---|---|---|---|---|
| 0 | × | 10 | = | 0 |
| 1 | × | 10 | = | 10 |
| 2 | × | 10 | = | 20 |
| 3 | × | 10 | = | 30 |
| 4 | × | 10 | = | 40 |
| 5 | × | 10 | = | 50 |
| 6 | × | 10 | = | 60 |
| 7 | × | 10 | = | 70 |
| 8 | × | 10 | = | 80 |
| 9 | × | 10 | = | 90 |
| 10 | × | 10 | = | 100 |
| 11 | × | 10 | = | 110 |
| 12 | × | 10 | = | 120 |

This is a telephone.

It has 10 numbers on it.

Here are another 9 telephones.

Each telephone has 10 numbers on it.

There are 10 telephones. Each telephone has 10 numbers.

How many numbers are there?

Answer: 10 telephones x 10 numbers = 100 numbers

**10 x 10 = 100**

---

If there were 11 rabbits and each rabbit had 10 carrots,

how many carrots would there be?

Answer: 11 rabbits x 10 carrots = 110 carrots **11 x 10 = 110**

**11 x 10 = 110** is the same as **10 x 11 = 110**

# 11 times table

| | | | |
|---:|:---:|:---:|---:|
| 0 | × | 11 = | 0 |
| 1 | × | 11 = | 11 |
| 2 | × | 11 = | 22 |
| 3 | × | 11 = | 33 |
| 4 | × | 11 = | 44 |
| 5 | × | 11 = | 55 |
| 6 | × | 11 = | 66 |
| 7 | × | 11 = | 77 |
| 8 | × | 11 = | 88 |
| 9 | × | 11 = | 99 |
| 10 | × | 11 = | 110 |
| 11 | × | 11 = | 121 |
| 12 | × | 11 = | 132 |

Here are 11 sweets.

Here are another 10 piles
each with 11 sweets.

There are 11 piles. Each pile has 11 sweets.

How many sweets are there?

Answer: 11 piles x 11 sweets = 121 sweets

**11 x 11 = 121**

---

If there were 12 ants and each ant had a pile of 11 seeds,
how many seeds would there be?

Answer: 12 ants x 11 seeds = 132 seeds     **12 x 11 = 132**

**12 x 11 = 132** is the same as **11 x 12 = 132**

# 12 times table

| | | | |
|---|---|---|---|
| 0 | × | 12 = | 0 |
| 1 | × | 12 = | 12 |
| 2 | × | 12 = | 24 |
| 3 | × | 12 = | 36 |
| 4 | × | 12 = | 48 |
| 5 | × | 12 = | 60 |
| 6 | × | 12 = | 72 |
| 7 | × | 12 = | 84 |
| 8 | × | 12 = | 96 |
| 9 | × | 12 = | 108 |
| 10 | × | 12 = | 120 |
| 11 | × | 12 = | 132 |
| 12 | × | 12 = | 144 |

This clock has 12 numbers on its face.

Here are another 11 clocks. Each clock has 12 numbers.

There are 12 clocks. Each clock has 12 numbers.

How many numbers can you see on the clocks?

Answer: 12 clocks x 12 numbers = 144 numbers

$$12 \times 12 = 144$$

---

If there were 7 snowflakes and each
snowflake had 12 points,

how many points would there be?

Answer: 7 snowflakes x 12 points = 84 points  $7 \times 12 = 84$
          $7 \times 12 = 84$ is the same as $12 \times 7 = 84$

## Times table sums

The answers are at the foot of the page

1)  2 boys: each boy has 7 balloons.
    How many balloons altogether?
    2 x 7 = ? 14

2)  3 monkeys: each monkey has 6 coconuts.
    How many coconuts altogether?
    3 x 6 = ? 18

3)  6 sheep: each sheep has 4 legs.
    How many legs in all?
    6 x 4 = ? 24

4)  4 mice: each mouse has 5 pieces of cheese.
    How many pieces of cheese altogether?
    4 x 5 = ? 20

5)  5 hens: each hen has laid 8 eggs.
    How many eggs in all?
    5 x 8 = ? 40

6)  7 octopuses: each octopus has 8 arms.
    How many arms altogether?
    7 x 8 = ? 56

6) 7 × 8 = **56**   5) 5 × 8 = **40**   4) 4 × 5 = **20**
3) 6 × 4 = **24**   2) 3 × 6 = **18**   1) 2 × 7 = **14**

# Times table sums

The answers are at the foot of the page

7) 9 flowers: each flower has 9 petals.
   How many petals in total?
   $9 \times 9 = ?$ 81

8) 8 puppies: each puppy has 9 balls.
   How many balls altogether?
   $8 \times 9 = ?$ 72

9) 7 rabbits: each rabbit has 5 carrots.
   How many carrots in all?
   $7 \times 5 = ?$ 35

10) 11 telephones: each phone has 10 numbers.
    How many numbers altogether?
    $11 \times 10 = ?$ 110

11) 9 plates: each plate has 4 chocolates on it.
    How many chocolates in all?
    $9 \times 4 = ?$ 36

12) 8 snowflakes: each snowflake has 12 points.
    How many points in total?
    $8 \times 12 = ?$ 96

7) $9 \times 6 = 81$    8) $8 \times 9 = 72$    9) $7 \times 5 = 35$

10) $11 \times 10 = 110$    11) $9 \times 4 = 36$    12) $8 \times 12 = 96$

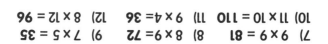

| | | |
|---|---|---|
| 0 x 1 = 0 | 0 x 2 = 0 | 0 x 3 = 0 |
| 1 x 1 = 1 | 1 x 2 = 2 | 1 x 3 = 3 |
| 2 x 1 = 2 | 2 x 2 = 4 | 2 x 3 = 6 |
| 3 x 1 = 3 | 3 x 2 = 6 | 3 x 3 = 9 |
| 4 x 1 = 4 | 4 x 2 = 8 | 4 x 3 = 12 |
| 5 x 1 = 5 | 5 x 2 = 10 | 5 x 3 = 15 |
| 6 x 1 = 6 | 6 x 2 = 12 | 6 x 3 = 18 |
| 7 x 1 = 7 | 7 x 2 = 14 | 7 x 3 = 21 |
| 8 x 1 = 8 | 8 x 2 = 16 | 8 x 3 = 24 |
| 9 x 1 = 9 | 9 x 2 = 18 | 9 x 3 = 27 |
| 10 x 1 = 10 | 10 x 2 = 20 | 10 x 3 = 30 |
| 11 x 1 = 11 | 11 x 2 = 22 | 11 x 3 = 33 |
| 12 x 1 = 12 | 12 x 2 = 24 | 12 x 3 = 36 |

| | | |
|---|---|---|
| 0 x 4 = 0 | 0 x 5 = 0 | 0 x 6 = 0 |
| 1 x 4 = 4 | 1 x 5 = 5 | 1 x 6 = 6 |
| 2 x 4 = 8 | 2 x 5 = 10 | 2 x 6 = 12 |
| 3 x 4 = 12 | 3 x 5 = 15 | 3 x 6 = 18 |
| 4 x 4 = 16 | 4 x 5 = 20 | 4 x 6 = 24 |
| 5 x 4 = 20 | 5 x 5 = 25 | 5 x 6 = 30 |
| 6 x 4 = 24 | 6 x 5 = 30 | 6 x 6 = 36 |
| 7 x 4 = 28 | 7 x 5 = 35 | 7 x 6 = 42 |
| 8 x 4 = 32 | 8 x 5 = 40 | 8 x 6 = 48 |
| 9 x 4 = 36 | 9 x 5 = 45 | 9 x 6 = 54 |
| 10 x 4 = 40 | 10 x 5 = 50 | 10 x 6 = 60 |
| 11 x 4 = 44 | 11 x 5 = 55 | 11 x 6 = 66 |
| 12 x 4 = 48 | 12 x 5 = 60 | 12 x 6 = 72 |